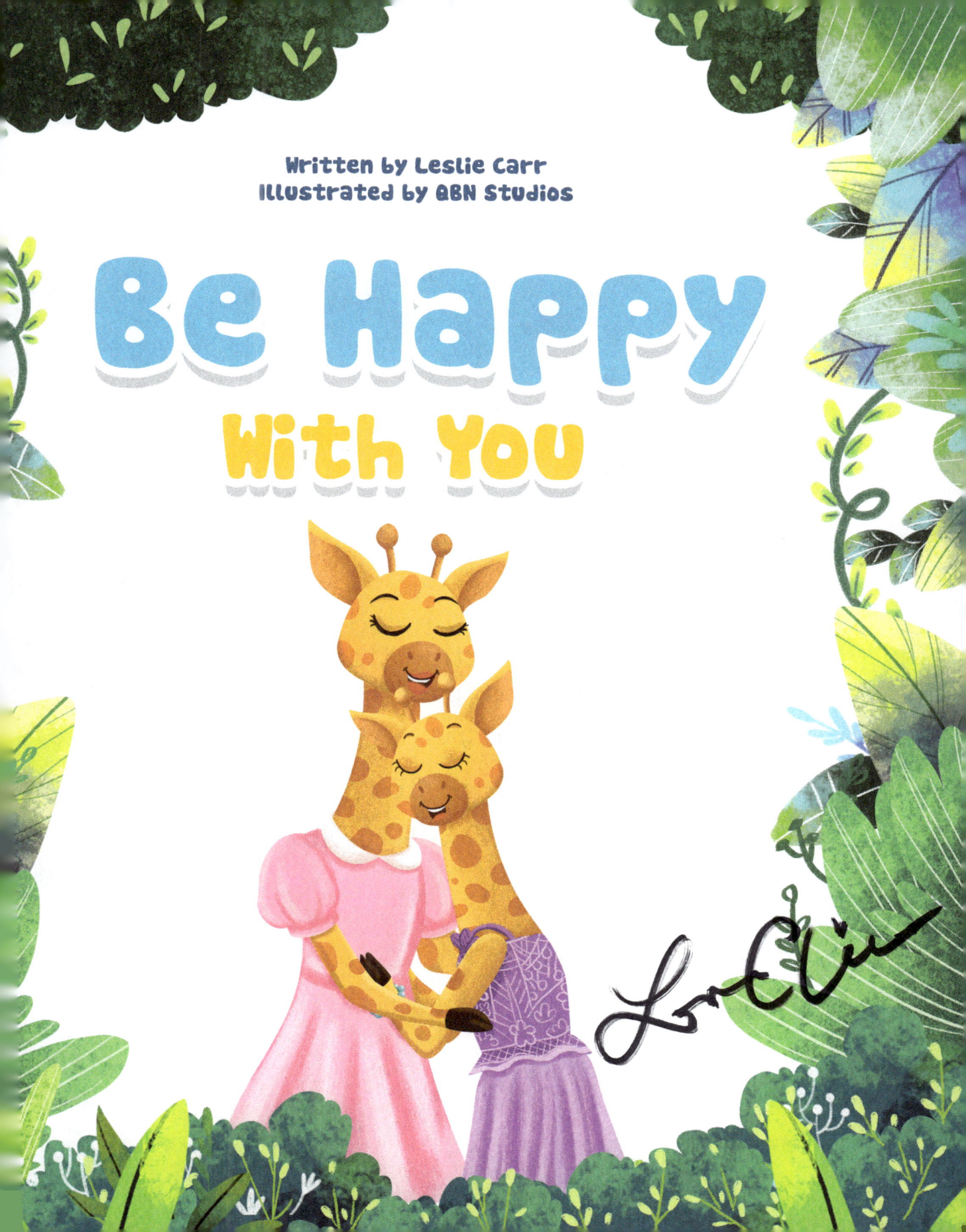

Written by Leslie Carr
Illustrated by QBN Studios

Be Happy
With You

Text copyright © 2022 by Leslie Carr

Illustrated by QBN Studios

All rights reserved. No part of this publication, including its characters, may be reproduced or transmitted in any form or by any means, electronic or mechanical, including photocopying, recording, or by information storage and retrieval system, without written permission of the author.

Paperback: 979-8-9867204-0-1

Ebook: 979-8-9867204-1-8

Hardcover: 979-8-9867204-2-5

Early Monday morning, the Giraffe family had just sat down for breakfast when out of the blue, Gabby had a question.

"Mom, why are we different from the other animals? I mean, why am I the tallest one in class?"

Gabby's mom replied with a smile "Because God made us all different for a reason."

"But why am I the tallest?"

"Someday, you will figure that out, and God will help you when he is ready" said Gabby's mom.

Gabby went off to school that day a little puzzled. She kept thinking "why did God create me to be the tallest kid in my class?"

At school, she looked at everyone in the classroom and everyone at recess. She loved watching everyone play. She loved it so much, that she had an idea.

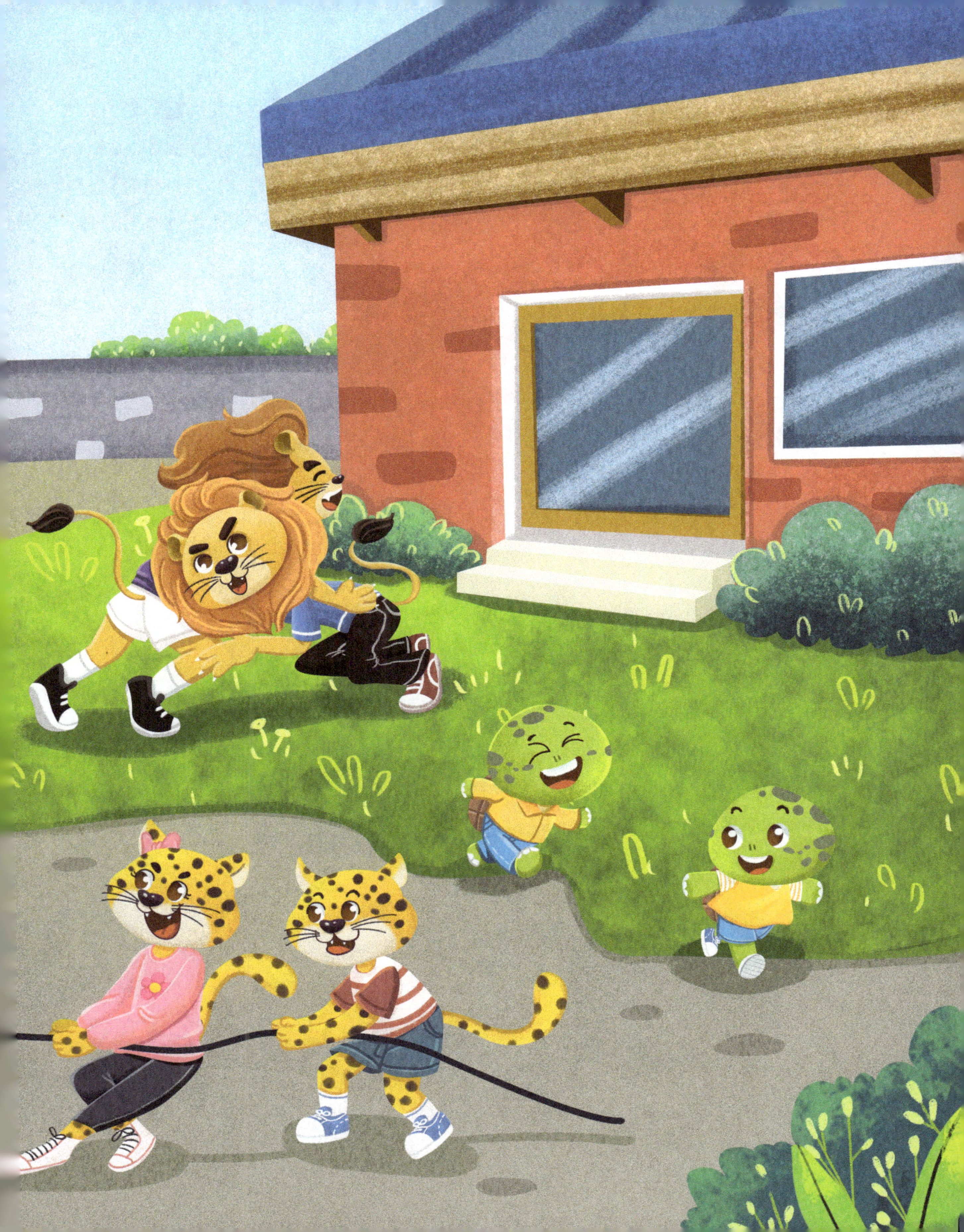

The next day, Gabby went to school with her cheetah printed tennis shoes on. Maybe if she wore them, she could run as fast as a cheetah! So, at recess, she asked if she could be in the foot race with them.

Charlie the Cheetah said "Sure Gabby! Line up!"

Gabby stood on the line with her long legs and tall stance which towered over the other cheetahs.

Charlie and the other racers crouched down in their speedy shorter legs position, ready for the time to go. Ozzy the Otter stood at the start line and yelled "Ready. Set. GO!"

And in just seconds, Gabby was left in a cloud of dust.

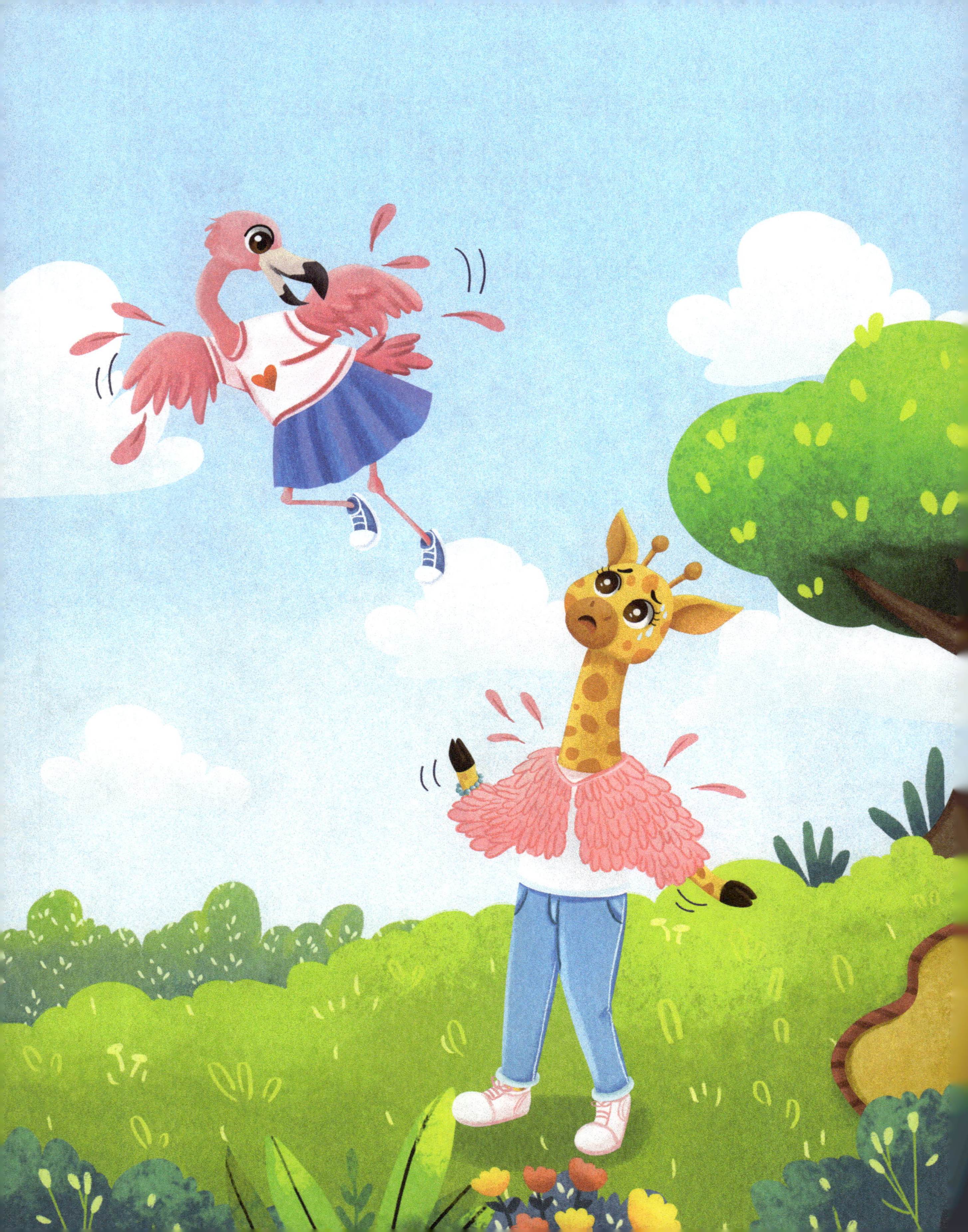

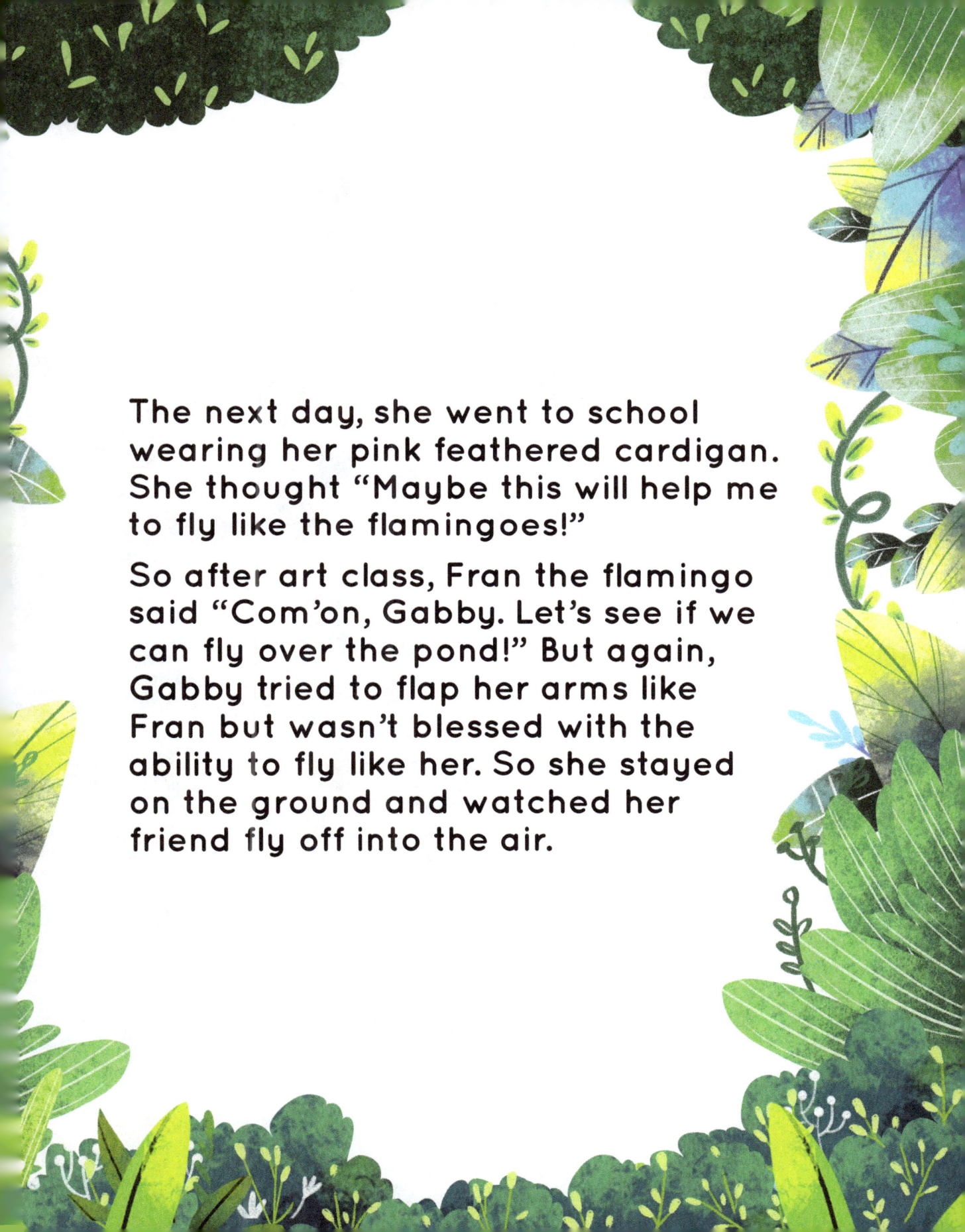

The next day, she went to school wearing her pink feathered cardigan. She thought "Maybe this will help me to fly like the flamingoes!"

So after art class, Fran the flamingo said "Com'on, Gabby. Let's see if we can fly over the pond!" But again, Gabby tried to flap her arms like Fran but wasn't blessed with the ability to fly like her. So she stayed on the ground and watched her friend fly off into the air.

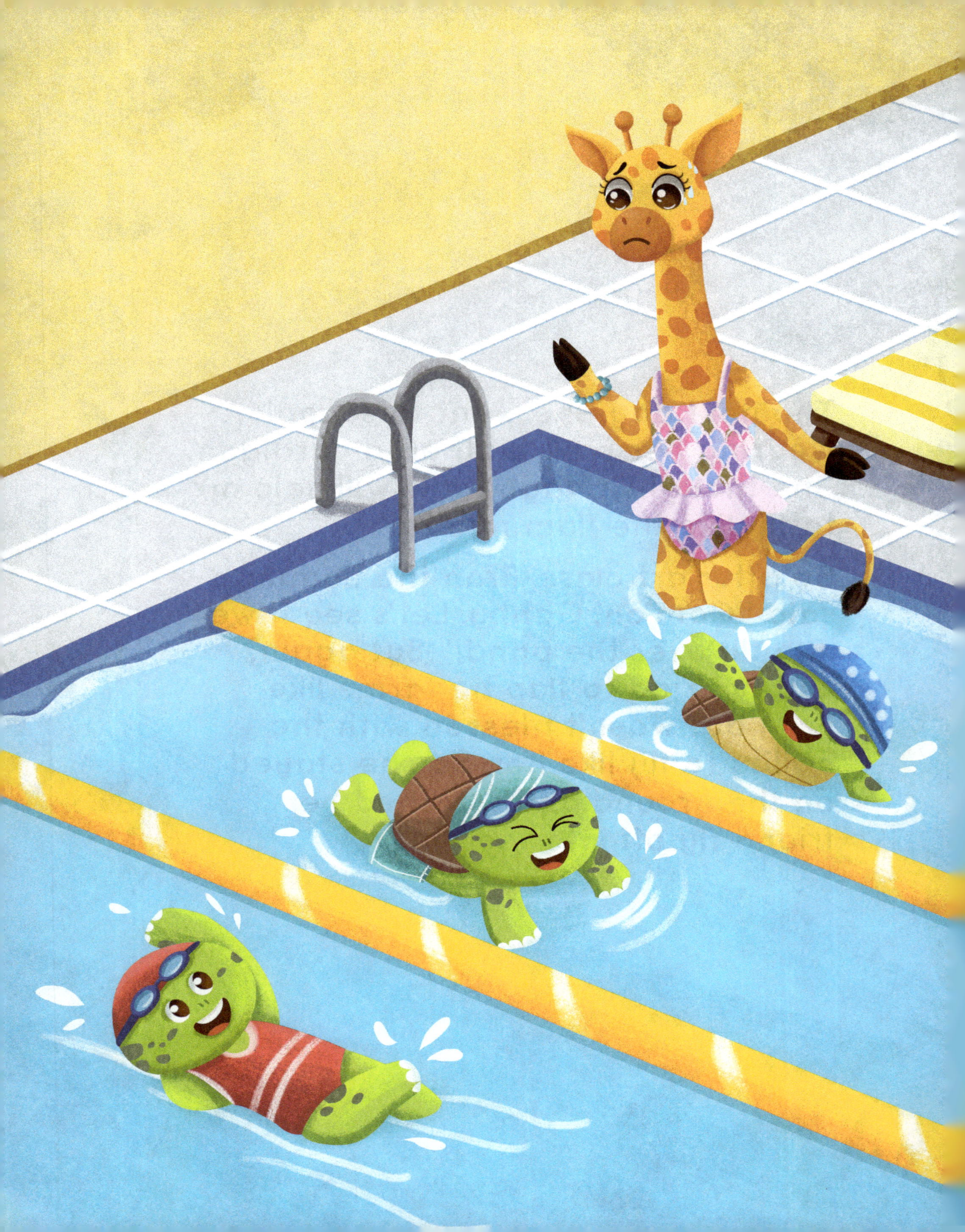

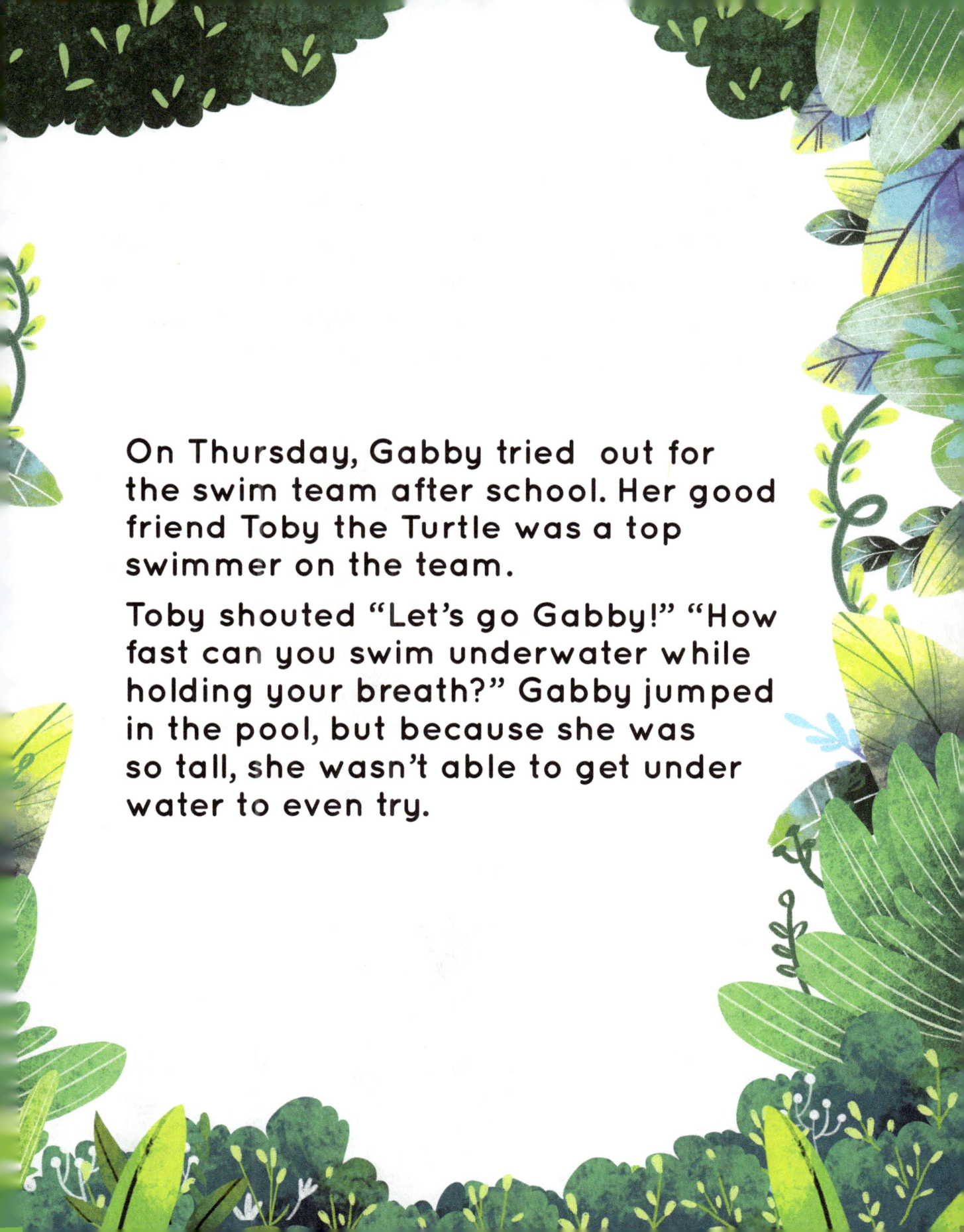

On Thursday, Gabby tried out for the swim team after school. Her good friend Toby the Turtle was a top swimmer on the team.

Toby shouted "Let's go Gabby!" "How fast can you swim underwater while holding your breath?" Gabby jumped in the pool, but because she was so tall, she wasn't able to get under water to even try.

That night, Gabby felt defeated. She still didn't know why she was the tallest and why she couldn't do all the same things as the other kids. All she wanted was to be like everyone else, but all she could hear was her mother saying "Be happy with you!"

The next day was Friday. They had a new student in class. Lettie, a lion cub. Everyone made sure to make Lettie feel welcome.

After lunch everyone went outside to play. Suddenly the tornado sirens went off as part of the monthly siren test. Everyone just went on playing...except Lettie! She ran right up the big oak tree in fright!

She was so scared, she didn't even realize how high up she had gone. When the teacher asked for her to come down, she couldn't move! She froze! Everyone looked around for help.

Charlie the cheetah tried climbing up the tree to help Lettie but because she climbed so far up, the branches started to break underneath him and he had to climb back down.

Next, Fran the flamingo flew up to try and help, but her wings started to get caught in the branches. So down she went without even getting close.

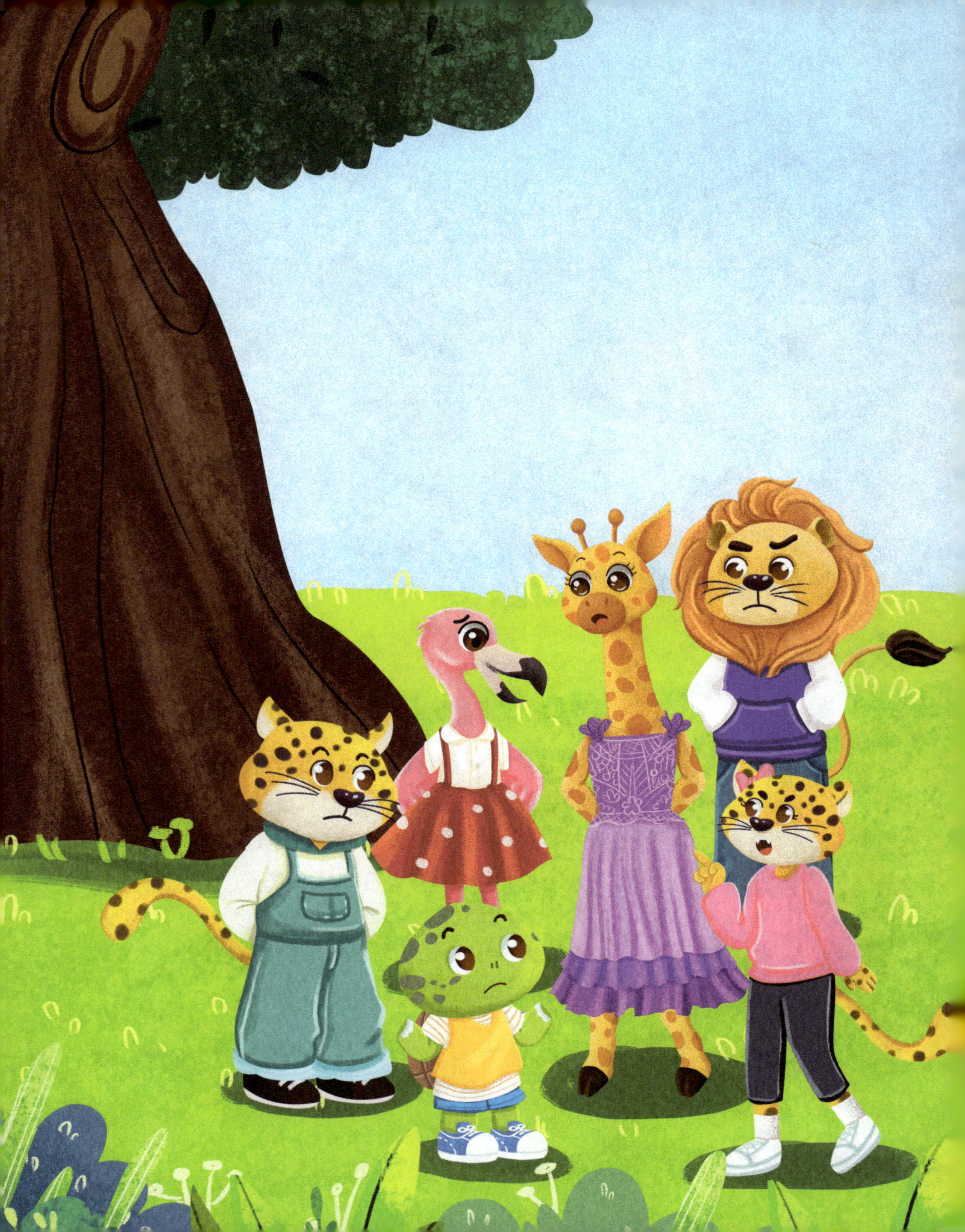

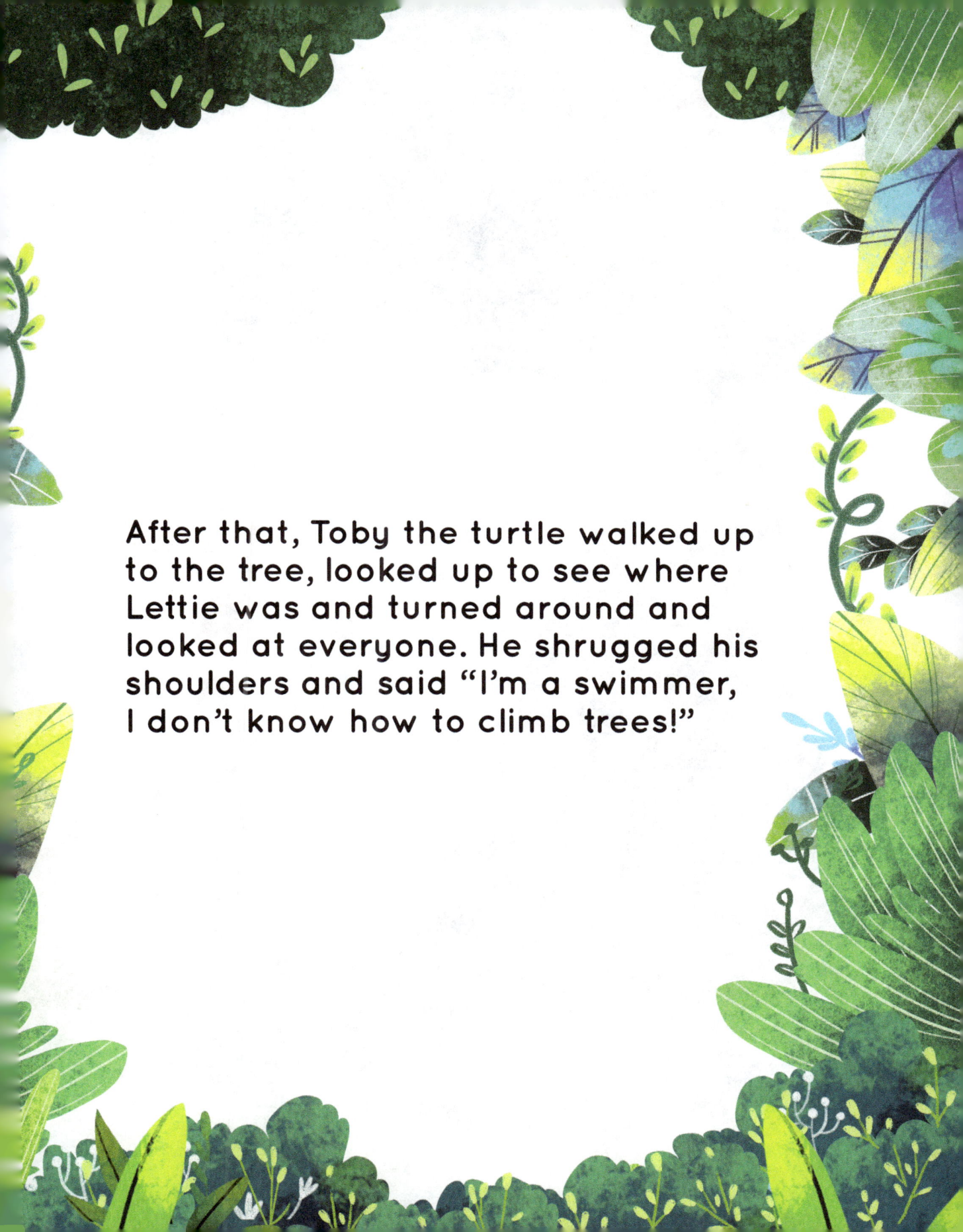

After that, Toby the turtle walked up to the tree, looked up to see where Lettie was and turned around and looked at everyone. He shrugged his shoulders and said "I'm a swimmer, I don't know how to climb trees!"

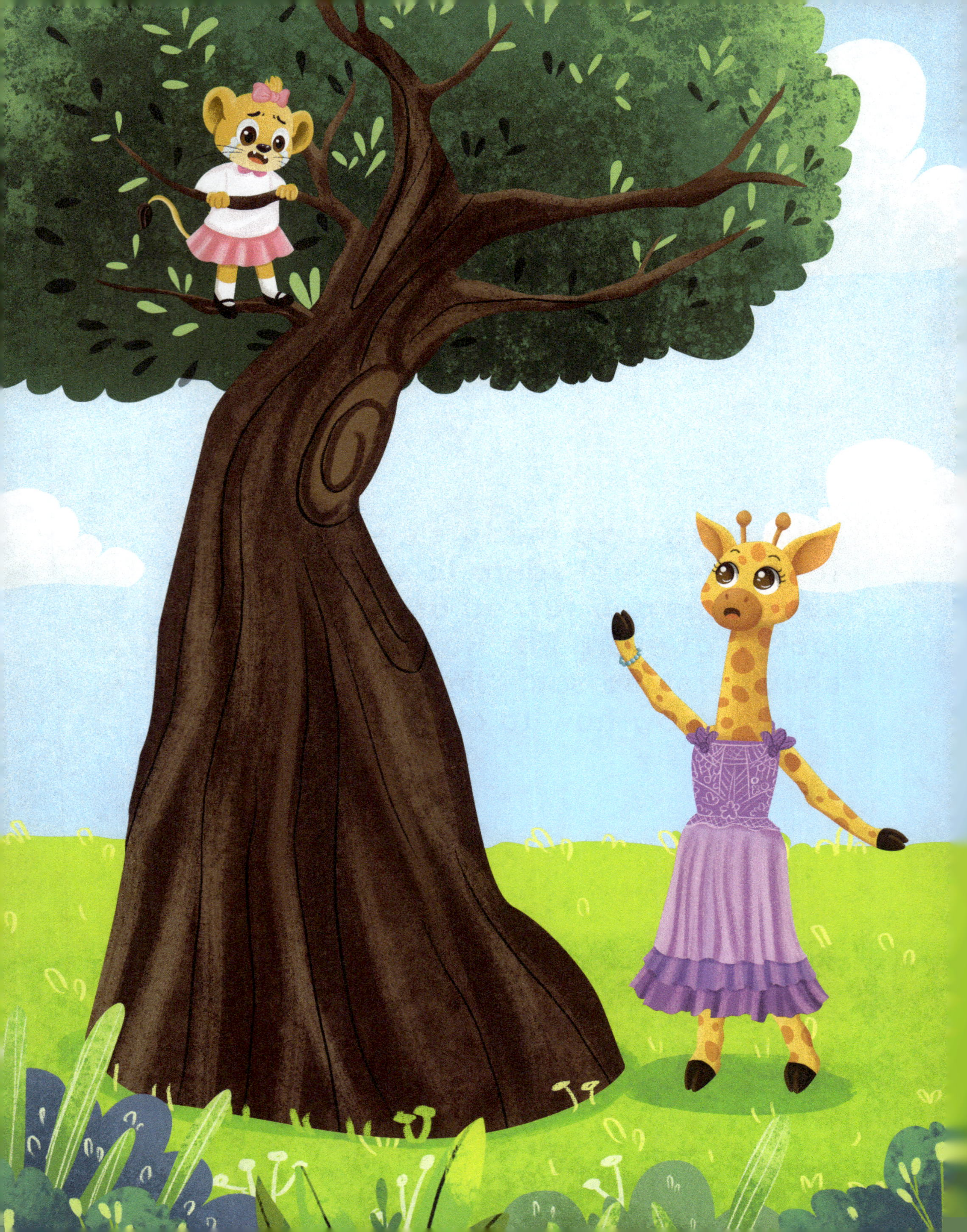

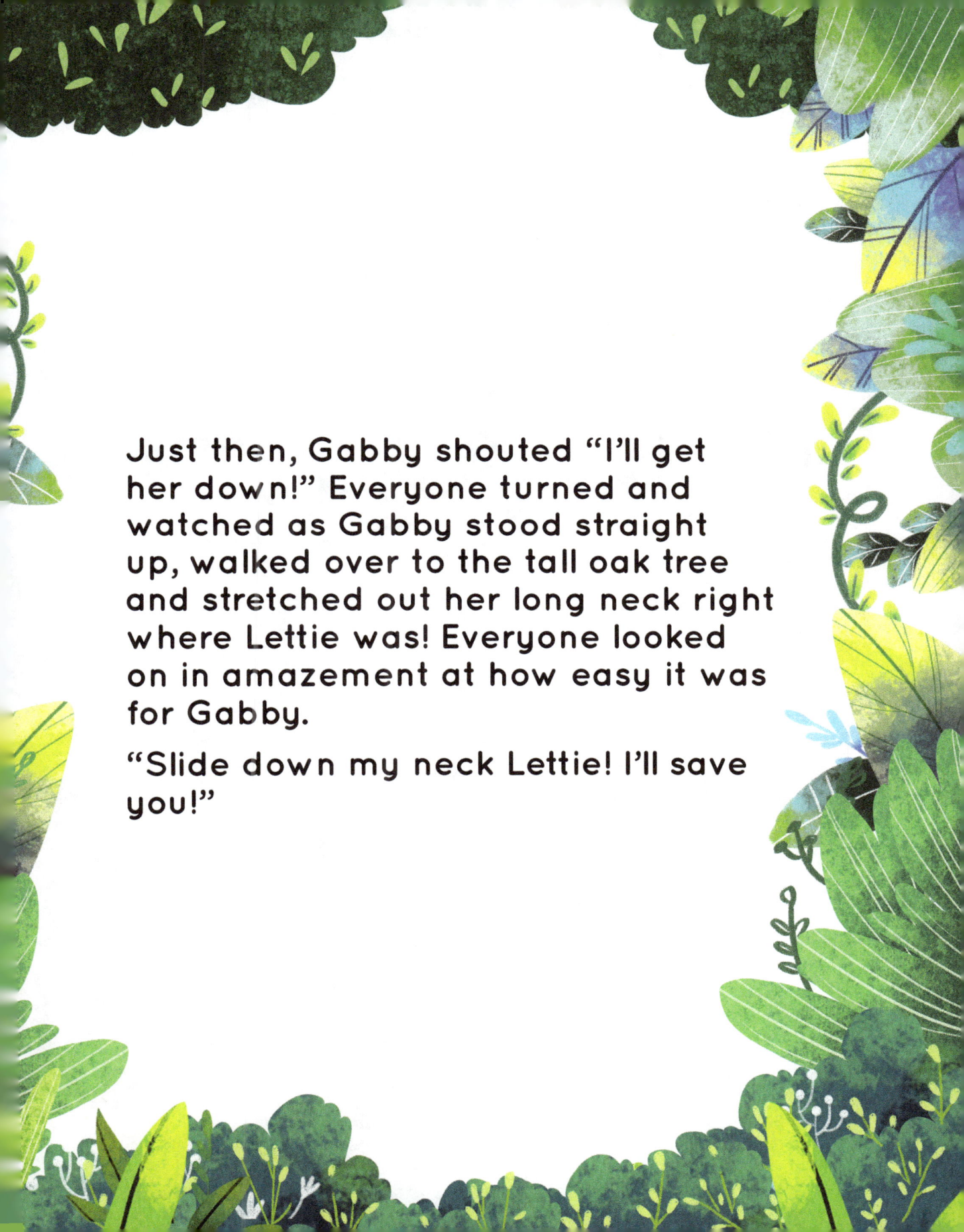

Just then, Gabby shouted "I'll get her down!" Everyone turned and watched as Gabby stood straight up, walked over to the tall oak tree and stretched out her long neck right where Lettie was! Everyone looked on in amazement at how easy it was for Gabby.

"Slide down my neck Lettie! I'll save you!"

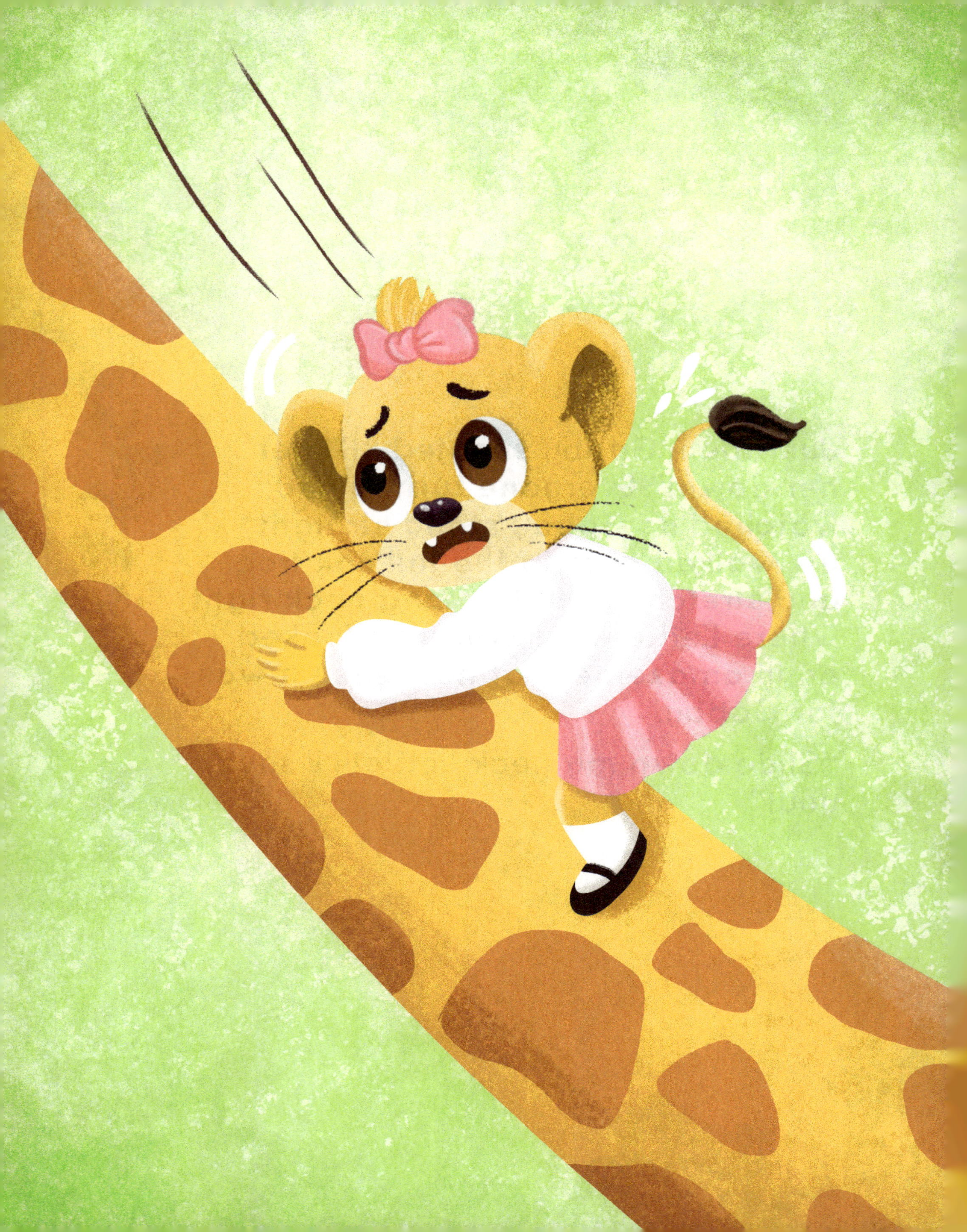

Lettie grabbed onto Gabby's neck and slid all the way down to safety!

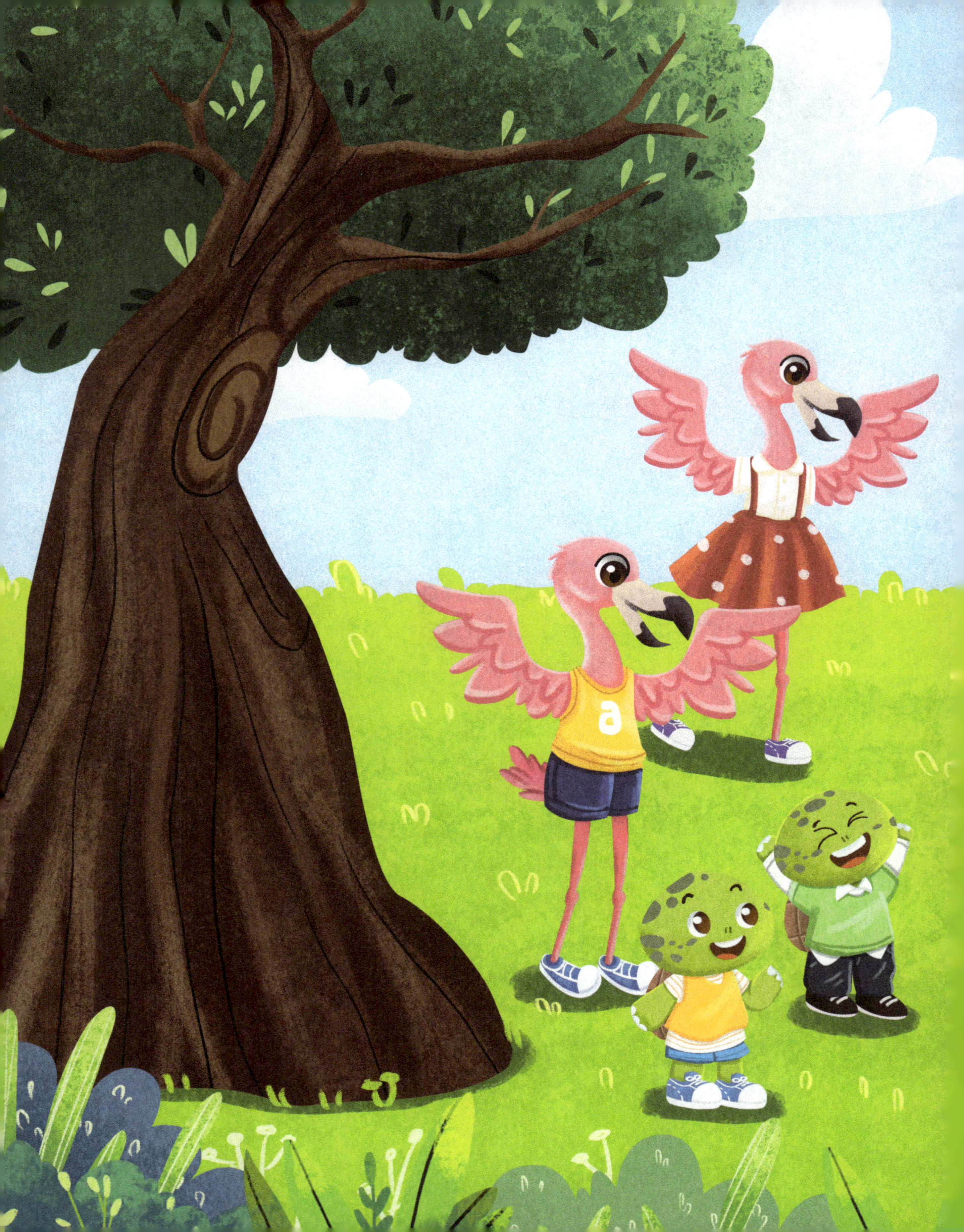

Everyone cheered as Gabby stood there with the biggest smile on her face, because she knew right then why God created her and although she was different from everyone else, she was happy with herself!

Author's Bio

Leslie Carr is a single mother of a beautiful 6 year old daughter named Willow. Willow is the inspiration behind Leslie's desire to write children's books. Be Happy With You is the result of a spontaneous request from Willow to her mom to make up an original story to tell her as she put her down for bed.

Leslie has a strong faith and a love for animals. Be Happy With You is a beautiful fusion of these two things to write a book that reflected the hope of God and the whimsical innocence of young animals.

Fascinated by children and how they piece together moments in their lives when things become challenging, Leslie's goal with writing is to bring a Godly perspective into the lives of children today by promoting faith and confidence.

CPSIA information can be obtained
at www.ICGtesting.com
Printed in the USA
LVHW020438240623
750695LV00006B/89